RECONSTRUCTION
And The New South
1865-1913

RECONSTRUCTION
And The New South
1865-1913

50 Essential Books

Clyde N. Wilson

SOUTHERN READER'S GUIDE III

SHOTWELL PUBLISHING
Columbia, South Carolina

Produced in the REPUBLIC OF SOUTH CAROLINA by

SHOTWELL PUBLISHING, LLC
Post Office Box 2592
Columbia, South Carolina 29202

www.ShotwellPublishing.com

Cover Image: "The Lost Cause" by Henry Mosler; oil on canvas, 1869. Courtesy WikiMedia Commons.
Cover Design: Hazel's Dream | Boo Jackson TCB

ISBN: 978-1-947660-23-6

10 9 8 7 6 5 4 3 2 1

For Don Livingston,

Torchbearer of the Southern Tradition

CONTENTS

INTRODUCTION

The first step in liquidating a people is to erase its memory. Destroy its books, its culture, its history. Then have somebody write new books, manufacture a new culture, invent a new history.
— Milan Kundera

The suffering that must exist in the South the next year . . . will be beyond conception. People who talk of further retaliation and punishment . . . do not conceive of the suffering endured already, or they are heartless.
—U.S. Grant, 1865

That the Southern people were put to the torture is vaguely understood, but even historians have shrunk from the unhappy task of showing us the torture chambers.... Never have American public men in responsible positions, directing the destiny of the nation, been so brutal, hypocritical, and corrupt.
—Claude G. Bowers of Indiana, popular historian of the 1920s and 1930s

... the most shameful decade in our entire national history. . .a moral collapse without precedent and, let us hope, without successor.... There is no parallel for the situation in the history of modern civilized nations, and it is almost incredible that it occurred within our own country.

—James Truslow Adams of New York, prominent historian of the 1920s and 1930s.

A great portion of our people have learned that they were being used as mere tools and determined by casting their ballots against these unprincipled adventurers, to overthrow them.

—Hiram Revels, African-American Senator from Mississippi

*　*　*

Reconstruction, 1865—1876

I find "Reconstruction" too sad and dreary a subject to urge anyone to read about it, but every good student of the South is obligated to understand this ugliest period of American history.

Historians in the early 20th century (the "Dunning School") for the first time approached Reconstruction with scholarly research and built up a factual account of the federal control of the South for ten years after The War. They documented that it was an orgy of stealing and oppression that spread disorder, looted the South of the resources needed to recover, left black and white Southerners antagonistic for the first time and worse off than they had ever been before, and unnecessarily created more bitterness than the war itself. (Imagine the kind of Northern thinking that turned the noble commonwealth of Virginia into Military District No. 1 and deprived the sons and grandsons of Revolutionary heroes of citizenship.)

William A. Dunning was a Northerner and a professor at Columbia University. He was the first serious scholarly investigator of the Reconstruction period. A number of his doctoral students were Southerners who wrote well-researched scholarly histories of what happened in various States.

Dunning and his students are today dismissed without reading by ideologically-driven historians and their acolytes.

Reconstruction was finally ended when the Northern public had become sufficiently ashamed and disgusted with corruption so pervasive that it reached high into President Grant's White House. In 1876 the Republicans agreed to remove the last troops supporting carpetbag governments in exchange for being allowed to steal the Presidential election from the Democrats. One wonders how repentant they were when Republican leaders continued to wave "the bloody shirt" and tried to make Generals Sherman and Sheridan (who wasn't even native born) into presidential candidates. And did nominate notoriously corrupt James A. Garfield and James G. Blaine.

Despite Lincoln's pretty words about "malice toward none," Reconstruction was motivated by Northern hatred and desire for revenge against Southerners and by the opportunity to exploit a conquered people for wealth by political corruption. At first Southerners were too busy trying to stay alive to put up much opposition.

"Reconstruction" had nothing to do with rebuilding a devastated region. Its aims were entirely the opposite of that. "Reconstruction" referred to "reconstructing" the Southern people according to the designs of the conquering Republican party, meanwhile using them as a money-making resource. In respect to hatred and the use of force Reconstruction policy resembled a revival of the reign of Oliver Cromwell. It can be argued that Reconstruction has never really ended.

Today the former scholarly interpretation of Reconstruction has been overtaken by a Marxist class conflict scenario: Reconstruction was a noble "unfinished revolution"—a struggle of African Americans and their friends to establish true equality and justice, which was ultimately defeated by vicious and violent Southern reactionaries. This is now the "mainstream" view. It is nothing but revolutionary romanticism, written by people who have no connection to or use for American history except in service to European-derived ideologies. It bears no relation to what black and white Southerners (or Northerners) lived during "Reconstruction." The basic false premise underlying this interpretation is that equality of the African American people was the goal of Reconstruction. But that never was a primary goal of those who orchestrated and profited from

Reconstruction and the invasion that preceded it. The goal was always to benefit Northerners. African Americans were just a means to that end.

Today the sufferings of Southerners in the War and Reconstruction do not even register on the national consciousness. How easy it is to endure other peoples' troubles! Several writers have recently attacked General Lee for being "bitter" after the war. How can one be bitter about his land and people being destroyed now that he has been shown the superior virtue of the other side? This is the same mentality that encourages Americans to wreak destructive havoc on other countries. Why don't they love us when we send drones half way around the world to blow up their weddings? After all, we mean well and only want to bring them good things.

Mainstream academic history has now almost universalised what is called "the Lost Cause Myth." According to this interpretation, everything favourable that may be said about the Confederacy is a lie made up by Southerners to cover up their sins. This only works if you start with the unexamined and often unconscious assumption that Southerners never tell the truth—that we are evil people and should not be allowed to speak for ourselves. It is tailor-made for petty intellectuals who have never performed the historian's basic duty of looking into the sources.

Like "the Lost Cause Myth," the interpretation of Reconstruction as "an unfinished revolution" now predominates in fashionable discourse. Yet, as long as people are free to investigate and think, interpretations of the past can change and sometimes they end up somewhere near where they were before.

Be on the watch for the next wave of academic propaganda that will assert that it has been proved that the war and Reconstruction were not really all that harmful to the South, and we lied about that too. This is untrue, but facts do not matter to people who follow the fashion makers. You heard it here first.

*   *   *

The New South, 1877—1913

Historians need periodisation—to divide the past into segments that may be descriptively handled. This good and necessary as long as we realise that it is a somewhat artificial imposition on reality. You cannot really set a day or even a year when the Industrial Revolution began, nor when Americans began to think about independence from Great Britain. But we can safely say that in some intangible sense the South began in the minds of 17th century English poets, as M.E. Bradford said, and has long continued in ways that may be demonstrated by facts and figures but are most importantly seen in a social soul that is shared "by those who have contributed to it" and have handed it down.

C. Vann Woodward famously defined a period of Southern history in his *Origins of the New South, 1877—1913*. In 1877 the last troops were withdrawn, some semblance of law and order and local government was re-established, and development of a way of life in radically changed circumstances was undertaken by millions of impoverished Southerners, black and white. In 1913, Woodrow Wilson, a President with Southern connections, took office and a friendly reunion of Northern and

Southern veterans took place at Gettysburg. It might be conveniently argued that the South at that point entered a new phase on the national scene.

The motif of "the New South" is generally portrayed as the adoption of Northern notions of economic development and money-making, as laid out in a famous speech by the Atlanta editor Henry W. Grady in 1886. There is a good deal of truth in this characterisation, although it should be made clear that in embracing the inevitable future Southerners by no means repudiated reverence for their Confederate heritage or intended to give up their own culture.

According to Woodward's interpretation Reconstruction ended when Southern elites ("Bourbons") made a deal with Big Business Republicans to keep their class power. Woodward was writing as a post-World War II Liberal who thought that an alliance between Republicans and Southern Democrats was holding back the further extension of the New Deal. It was considered historical background for what progressives saw as happening in their own time.

You can find some evidence for this thesis, but it under-estimates the continuing strength of the Jeffersonian tradition among Southern leaders and spokesmen. Serious opposition to the power of Big Business and Big Banking remained strongest in the South. Southern opposition to American imperialism in the Spanish American War, Hawaiian revolution, and WW I was considerable and on Jeffersonian grounds. The significant persistence of Jeffersonianism and rejection of the state capitalism of "the Great Barbecue" among Southern people and leaders deserves more serious study than it has yet received.

The "New South" period is also that of the Progressive Era of American history, marked by the increasing force of top-down reforms that collectivised much of society and gave decision-making power to "experts." Despite historians' fondness for characterising the South in this period as "reactionary," Southerners, in the midst of their poverty, participated in "progressivism" in their own way: tariff reduction, farm co-operatives, better educational opportunity for white and black, regulation of railroads (which were, after all, built with government money) and farm-to-market roads.

Toward the later 19th century there developed a spirit of reconciliation between North and South that persisted until past the bicentennial of the

1960s but is now wholly obliterated. Southerners agreed they were glad "the Union" had been preserved and promised to defend it faithfully. Northerners agreed that the war had honourable and sincere men on both sides and that Confederate heroes were American heroes. Only our side has kept the bargain

Northern views of the South, whether malicious propaganda or a fondness for "moonlight and magnolias," have always served Northern purposes, as does today's "Confederaphobia." Until the 1850s, when new economic and cultural forces led an aggressive North to seize the power and the idea of America, the South and "America" were one and the same. The South has since been "the Internal Other," seen not for itself but in whatever way is useful for the Northern psyche. The Southern writers (like Thomas Nelson Page) who wrote charming accounts (now derided) of the South in the late 19th and early 20th centuries could not have succeeded so well if they had not gratified Northern readers. The Yankee elite, made uneasy by immigrants and labour unrest, found comfort in reading of an earlier and very American time and region — un-urbanised, unindustrialised, with Anglo-Saxons firmly in control.

During the period of the "New South" the Southern people enjoyed some economic development, regained a measure of political power, and preserved and expanded their own culture in manners, music, and literature. But, it should not be forgotten that the South experienced mass poverty and intractable race problems while the nearly all-white North, generally speaking, enjoyed prosperity, progress, and optimism.

Clyde N. Wilson
Dutch Fork, Republic of South Carolina

I. RECONSTRUCTION

1.

Southern Reconstruction (2017)
by Philip Leigh

Given the prevailing interpretations in our time of Reconstruction, the appearance of this solid, truthful instant classic is nearly a miracle. It is the first even-handed treatment of the tangled question of Reconstruction that has appeared in some years and has raised the author to the front rank of scholars of the period. With penetrating research and insight, Leigh tells the real factual history of Reconstruction oppression and corruption. A book that should be on every American bookshelf. Among the many merits of Leigh's work is the recognition that "Reconstruction" was national and that it was harmful to both white and black Southerners in ways that continued long after the end of Political Reconstruction in 1876.

2.

North Against South:
The American Iliad, 1848—1877
by Ludwell H. Johnson

This is a book that should be read and re-read and digested by every American who wants to understand the causes, conduct, and results of the War Between the States. Most of the writing and general public knowledge of the central event in American history rests upon a Northern viewpoint —the South is to be understood as provoking war by resistance to a benevolent government in unforgivable defense of slavery. Written with strict professional historianship and superb mastery of the sources and literature, *North Against South* tells a different story—not by defending the South but by close examination of the motives and actions of the North. Ludwell Johnson was a Virginian with a Ph.D. from Johns Hopkins University and a long-time popular professor of history at William and Mary College. The book originally appeared under the title *Division and Reunion: America, 1844—1877*. Johnson's discussion of the historiography of "Reconstruction" is a must read.

3.

The Story of Reconstruction (1938)
by Robert Selph Henry

This lively popular history survey of the Reconstruction era in American history, by the author of *The Story of the Confederacy*, is a good place to begin reading for a general overview. See *The War Between the States: 60 Essential Books, no.* 3 for more about the author.

4.

The South During Reconstruction (1947)
by E. Merton Coulter

Coulter (1890—1981) was once widely recognised as a leading historian of the South. He was Professor of History at the University of Georgia for many years, the author of 26 worthy books on Southern history, and the first president of the Southern Historical Association. His substantial study of Reconstruction is a scholarly account based on extensive research. It is filled with details that do not appear in recent "mainstream" justifications of Reconstruction and therefore remains of real interest to students of Southern history.

5.

The Southern States Since the War (1871)
by Robert Somers

An English visitor's unbiased and illuminating first-hand description of the anarchy and despotism of Congressional Reconstruction.

6.

The Prostrate State: South Carolina Under Negro Government (1874)
by James S. Pike

A veteran journalist's first-hand report of the evils of Reconstruction in South Carolina. Made all the more telling because Pike was born in Maine, was an abolitionist and Radical Republican, and received a diplomatic appointment from Lincoln.

7.

Reconstruction: Political and Economic, 1865–1877 (1907)
by William A. Dunning

William A. Dunning (1857—1922) was Northern born and raised and a longtime distinguished professor of history and political philosophy at Columbia University at a time when it was the leading producer of professional scholars in the U.S. Dunning was authoritative on many subjects and his Reconstruction book was the first attempt to present a scholarly and factual account without partisanship. Though now anathema, in its time it was widely praised for its "meticulous and thorough research," avoidance of the common polemics of historical writing at the time, and effort to establish objective truth. Dunning directed the PhD work of students, many from the South, who wrote histories of Reconstruction in individual States.

8.
The "Dunning School"
State Histories of Reconstruction

These books, published in the early 20th century, began as doctoral dissertations under William A. Dunning at Columbia University in New York. They are uneven in quality but all are full of the kinds of facts that go unnoticed today: J.W. Garner on Mississippi; Walter L. Fleming on Alabama; Mildred C. Thompson on Georgia; J.S. Reynolds on South Carolina; W.W. Davis on Florida; J.G. deRoulhac Hamilton on North Carolina; Charles W. Ramsdell on Texas. Not of the Dunning School and of a later date but relevant is E. Merton Coulter, *Civil War and Readjustment in Kentucky*. While these works (with great justice) identify carpetbaggers as the main villains in Reconstruction, they do not spare showing the bad deeds of Southerners where appropriate.

9.

The Tragic Era:
The Revolution After Lincoln (1929)
by Claude G. Bowers

Bowers (1878—1958) was from Indiana and was a very widely read popular historian, most of his work being a celebration of the Democratic Party. (FDR appointed him ambassador to Spain.) The goodness of the Democrats and the evil of their opponents marked his books on the Jeffersonian and Jacksonian eras. The chief value of his Reconstruction book is in his defense of Andrew Johnson and his vivid portrayals of the evil perpetrators of Reconstruction like Thaddeus Stevens and Charles Sumner.

10.

The Invisible Empire: The Story of
the Ku Klux Klan, 1866—1871 (1939)
by Stanley F. Horn

Stanley F. Horn (1889—1980) was a Tennessee businessman and editor and quite a good popular historian. (See *The War Between the States: 60 Essential Books*, no. 37 for more on the author.) This book treats the necessity of the *original* KKK and the respectability of its leaders, providing a lot of now unnoticed information.

11.

Washington's KKK: The Union League During Southern Reconstruction
by John Chodes

Present-day interpretation of Reconstruction as an "unfinished revolution" postulates that a supposed Southern "ruling class" engaged in concerted violence to suppress the freedom of African-Americans. There are a number of things wrong with this, including bypassing the question of who initiated violence. As Chodes's study makes clear, it was the abuses of the militarised, secretive carpetbagger-led black Union League that destroyed Southern whites' peaceful acceptance of black emancipation and their friendly co-operation with the freed people. In parts of the South, the imposed "legal" authority became a threat to life and property, which prompted a very American vigilante response. In places where the abuses were not so great, the Klan did not appear and it was dissolved as soon as law and order was re-established.

12.

Dixie After the War (1906)
by Myrta Lockett Avary

Myrta Lockett Avary (1857—1946) grew up in Virginia during Reconstruction. She became a successful journalist in New York. In 1903 she published *A Virginia Girl in the Civil War*, which was nationally popular. At public urging she followed with *Dixie After the War*. She declared her intention in the book to provide "the kind of history a witness gives" about Southern life "during the twelve years succeeding the fall of Richmond." The book is made up of the accounts of "observers and participants" of the time "brought together in one book for the first time." This is "Reconstruction" as Southerners lived it day by day.

13.

Gone With the Wind (1936)
by Margaret Mitchell

Of course, no Southern list of books on Reconstruction can overlook this Southern icon. There is a familiar story that the author had stuffed her couch with the manuscript. When a New York literary agent visited Atlanta she got it out. The result was in its time *the* top international best-seller, translated into every language in which books were printed and turned into an all-time blockbuster movie. Although *Gone With the Wind* has some soap opera elements, it is also a true picture of what Southerners suffered in The War and "Reconstruction," just as the author intended. Re-reading the work after some years, I gained an increased respect for its literary quality, an experience in which I am not alone. When Miss Scarlett vowed from the bare red clay field of Tara that she and her folks would never starve again, she epitomised for all time what the South faced in defeat and Reconstruction.

14.

The Sequel of Appomattox:
A Chronicle of the Reunion of the States (1918)
by Walter Lynwood Fleming

Near the end of World War I, Yale University commissioned a 50-volume series, *Chronicles of America*, designed to cover American political, economic, and social history. Readers familiar with today's historiography will be amazed to find that the volume dealing with Reconstruction was assigned to Walter Lynwood Fleming (1874—1942), a native of Alabama and professor at Vanderbilt University. They will also be surprised, perhaps, to find a straightforward, concise, factual account of the various aspects of the period that is still useful. When Woodrow Wilson was president of Princeton University he tried unsuccessfully to lure Fleming to his faculty. Those familiar with the Twelve Southerners of *I'll Take My Stand* might note that they dedicated their book to Fleming —with "love, admiration" and "perfect esteem." Fleming's history of Reconstruction in Alabama is one of the best of State histories for the period. Undaunted readers should also look at Dunning's collection *Documentary History of Reconstruction*, 2 vols., 1906.

15.
U.S. Grant's Failed Presidency (2019)
by Phillip Leigh

Leigh, the most outstanding recent historian of Reconstruction gives chapter and verse of the corruption of the Reconstruction President and shows the fallacy of recent efforts to see him as a "civil rights" promoter.

16.

Bloodstains: An Epic History of the Politics that Produced the American Civil War: Volume 4, Political Reconstruction and the Struggle for Healing
by Howard Ray White

The final volume of White's unique series covers the postwar period. As the author makes clear, while Political Reconstruction ended in 1876, reconciliation ("healing") only began with the election as President of the Democrat Grover Cleveland in 1884. Like White's other volumes, this book is dense with valuable material about the period and its principal characters during and after the War Between the States—a treasury of solid knowledge nowhere else brought together.

17.

Why the Solid South?, or Reconstruction and its Results (1890)
Edited by Hilary A. Herbert

Hilary Abner Herbert (1834—1919) was a Confederate colonel and after the war was a prolific author, Representative from Alabama, and U.S. Secretary of the Navy under Grover Cleveland. Why was the South solidly Democratic and lacking a two-party system like the rest of the country? Herbert explains this to those who ask the question.

18.

St. Elmo (1866)
by Augusta Jane Evans

St. Elmo was a spectacular bestseller in its time, rivaling Northerners' *Uncle Tom's Cabin* and *Ben-Hur*. It sold a million copies in its first four months, obviously presenting a theme that resonated strongly at the time. *St. Elmo* was produced on stage and in several early silent movies, and became a household term, a name for towns, hotels, steamboats, a cigar brand, and much else. Tastes and morals have changed since this work was written, but it has a modern theme—the romantic conflict between a cynical man and a devout woman. It certainly constitutes a rejoinder to the common claim that Southern culture and literature were insular and unimportant at the time. Augusta Jane Evans (1835-1909), (Mrs. Lorenzo M. Wilson of Columbus, Georgia), was a gifted writer, deserving to be much better known by real students of the South. As important, or more important than *St. Elmo* are her novels *Beulah* (1859) and *Macaria* (1864).

Copies of the latter were destroyed when found in the possession of Union soldiers. For more about the author see *The War Between the States: 60 Essential Books*, no. 21.

19.

New Orleans: The Place and the People (1895)
by Grace King

Grace Elizabeth King (1852-1932) of New Orleans is among the most important literary voices of the South in her time, along with Thomas Nelson Page, Joel Chandler Harris, and Mary Johnston.* King was equally accomplished and prolific in fiction and non-fiction. *Balcony Stories*, perhaps her most important fiction, contains realistic stories of the struggles of women in difficult circumstances. This work might be considered a landmark of genuine feminism (as opposed to the ideological sort). Her history of America's most unique city from its beginnings is based upon good historical study and personal experience. Among many other virtues, the author lived through Reconstruction in New Orleans and portrays the true history that has now been largely replaced by a Politically Correct version. Also of interest is her *Memories of a Southern*

Woman of Letters (1932). [*For Mary Johnston see
Southern Reader's Guide 2: The War Between the States,
no. 10.]

*　　*　　*

II. THE NEW SOUTH
(1877-1913)

20.

Punished with Poverty: The Suffering South (2016)

by James Ronald Kennedy & Walter Donald Kennedy

"It is true we are completely under the saddle of Massachusetts and Connecticut," wrote Thomas Jefferson in 1798, "and that they ride us very hard, cruelly insulting our feelings, as well as exhausting our strength and substance." Jefferson was asking whether joining New England in the common government of the United States had not become a bad bargain for the South. Through the colonial period and into the early 19th century, the South was prosperous. Since then, with tariffs and North-favouring expenditures, destruction by invasion, Reconstruction looting, and partial legislation, Southerners, black and white, have been, and still are, up to the present moment, the poorest Americans—and Southern "feelings" suffer from constant denunciation for being out-of-step in religion and values from the rest of the U.S. The Kennedy brothers, long known as fearless spokesman for the Southern people, have written an original and important contribution to Southern history. They relate the long story of the poverty *imposed* on the South.

21.

The Road to Reunion, 1865—1900 (1938)
by Paul H. Buck

Paul Herman Buck (1899—1978) was a native of Ohio and a long-time professor at Harvard University. He won the Pulitzer Prize for this book. Those who are familiar with present day writings on the South after the war and with current anti-Confederate hysteria will probably be surprised at his treatment of the subject. By 1900 decent Northerners had come to accept Southerners as valuable fellow countrymen, while former Confederates sat in Presidents' cabinets and on the U.S. Supreme Court. In 1900, and at the time Buck wrote, believe it or not, this was near universally considered a very good thing. Americans of North and South were reconciled in patriotic spirit and reverence for their dead, although in politics Republicans continued to wave the "bloody shirt."

22.

The South to Posterity: An Introduction to the Writings of Confederate History
by Douglas Southall Freeman

The Virginian Freeman was well-known for his Pulitzer Prize winning works *R.E. Lee* and *Lee's Lieutenants*. In *The South to Posterity* he provides a useful guide to the writings of former Confederates after the war. For more on Freeman see *The War Between the States: 60 Essential Books*, no. 22.

23.

The Creed of the Old South (1915)
by Basil L. Gildersleeve

Gildersleeve (1831—1924) was a native of Charleston and in 1851 was one of the first Americans to receive a doctorate from a German University. A professor of Classics at the University of Virginia and later Johns Hopkins University, he was also a Confederate soldier wounded in action. Gildersleeve's work was so important that he is still regarded in both the U.S. and Europe as the foremost American classical scholar of all time. Far from being a stuffy scholar, Gildersleeve made the classics come alive and he was a graceful essayist on matters not related to his profession. These writings were a contribution to healing the wounds of war. The war, said Gildersleeve, was a dispute over grammar —whether the United States *is* or the United States *are*. The latter was the creed of the Old South.

24.
The Southern Tradition at Bay
by Richard M. Weaver

This work was Weaver's PhD dissertation in 1943 under Cleanth Brooks at Louisiana State University, not published until 46 years later, posthumously. Weaver surveys the thinkers who continued to defend the values of Southern culture during the materialistic era after the War for Southern Independence and why they did so.

25.
Origins of the New South, 1877—1913
by C. Vann Woodward

Woodward (1908—1999) was a native of Arkansas and long-time professor at Yale University. Given the intellectual climate of his time, it is obvious that he could not have been the most acclaimed and rewarded Southern historian of the 20th century if he had expressed a Southern viewpoint. However, Woodward, although he used his talents in service of "liberal" opinion, was an ironic and complicated writer. You might say that while he was a critic of the South he never bought completely into its counterpart—Northern righteousness. That stance is reflected in *Origins of the New South, 1877—1913*. This book makes a good framework for study of its time and contains much useful and interesting matter. Woodward's more celebrated works, like *Reunion and Reaction* and *The Strange Career of Jim Crow* have been seriously challenged by other historians, but *The Burden of Southern History* and *American Counterpoint* are still of interest.

26.

Up from Slavery: An Autobiography (1900)
by Booker T. Washington

In one of the most important autobiographies in American literature, Booker Taliaferro Washington (1856-1915) tells the story of his life. He was born the property of a small slaveholder, heroically struggled for an education, and became a leader of the African American people and their spokesman to the mighty of American society. Washington's other books, like *The Story of the Negro: The Rise of the Race from Slavery* (1909), are valuable sources for the time.

27.

Chronicles of Chicora Wood
and A Woman Rice Planter
by Elizabeth Allston Pringle

The widow Elizabeth Allston Pringle (1845—1921) made a life in the post-Reconstruction South as a rice planter in the Lowcountry of South Carolina. She was one of the last in a way of life that was wrecked by the war and hurricanes. Her recollections of living and working in a rural area mostly populated by African Americans, are an important view of a neglected time and place and also the record of an extraordinary woman. Her sketches of plantation life were first published in national journals under the pseudonym "Patience Pennington." They became a book in 1913 with memorable art work by Alice Ravenel Huger Smith. Although published later and posthumously, *Chronicles of Chicora Wood* relates the experiences of a widow in Reconstruction. Also of interest is

Pringle's *Rab and Dab,* about two abandoned African American boys that she took responsibility for.

28.

Charles Goodnight,
Cowman and Plainsman (1936)
by J. Evetts Haley

Haley (1901—1995), was a Texas cattleman and also an accomplished historian of the American West. This biography records a great phase of Southern history —the creation of the Texas cattle kingdom. Charles Goodnight (1836—1929) was a Texas Ranger, Confederate soldier, and trail-blazer. He played a major role, along with others, in developing the drive of Texas longhorns to the North and in expanding the cattle kingdom into new territory. In the time and circumstances in which he lived, those who knew him regarded him as a great man. (It is said that Woodrow Call in "Lonesome Dove" is modeled on Goodnight, not very accurately.)

29.

Discussions: Secular (1897)
by Robert Lewis Dabney

Robert Lewis Dabney (1820—1898) is still known as a brilliant Presbyterian theologian and preacher and a friend and biographer of Stonewall Jackson. More relevant to our purpose here, Dabney was an eloquent public voice of the unreconstructed South from the War Between the States to the end of the 19th century. Dabney told Southerners that, although their cause was lost, it was right and they should never yield that point to the enemy. He was an effective critic of the world the Yankees were creating after the war in ways that may seem to be prophetic. In these collected writings, from the standpoint of the Old South, Dabney pointed to the social evils of secular public schools, Yankee capitalist greed, superficial culture, unsound money, and the materialism, lack of spirituality and atheism that were flourishing in the later 19th century. *Discussions: Secular* is vol. 4 of a collection of Dabney's writings edited by C.R. Vaughan. This book, along with other of Dabney's works, has been reprinted by Sprinkle Publications of Harrisonburg, Virginia.

30.

Lady Baltimore (1906) and *The Virginian* (1902)
by Owen Wister

Owen Wister (1860—1938) was a socially prominent Philadelphian and a friend of Theodore Roosevelt and other notable people of his time. He is most famous for his novel *The Virginian*, published in 1902 and regarded as the foundational work of serious Western fiction. That the hero of this first Western novel, set in Wyoming, is called "The Virginian" suggests the predominant role of the South in settling the West. *Lady Baltimore* takes place in Charleston. Wister contrasts the quietly admirable qualities and standards of the impoverished Charleston gentry with the doubtful character of visiting new-rich Northerners. Like a host of other outsiders, Wister found the South to be a valuable and congenial part of America.

31.

The American Negro: What He Was, What He Is, and What He May Become (1901)
by William Hannibal Thomas

William Hannibal Thomas (1843—1935) was born in Ohio as a free African American. He was an officer of U.S. Colored Troops in the War Between the States in which he lost an arm. At various times he was a teacher, theology student, member of the South Carolina legislature during Reconstruction, journal editor, and a U.S. Consul in Africa. He wrote this intensive work, realistically assessing what he observed to be the situation and future of his people in the U.S. His work, which carried the subtitle *A Critical and Practical Discussion*, was attacked by other prominent black leaders as too negative and as laying too much responsibility on African Americans for their condition.

32.

Colonel Carter of Cartersville (1891)
by F. Hopkinson Smith

Francis Hopkinson Smith (1838—1915) of Maryland was a prolific and quite popular author of his time. He was also a still-recognised artist and an engineer of important projects. This work portrays the "Southern Colonel" of the post-War Between the States period, long a popular figure in American folklore up until the recent present. The "Southern Colonel" is generally likable although occasionally considered a little bit laughable for his old-fashioned manners, chivalric integrity, and out-dated eloquence of speech. Not great literature but a pleasant read.

33.
The Search for Order, 1877—1920
by Robert H. Wiebe

This book is not particularly Southern-oriented but it is an expert guide to understanding the "Progressive Era" of American history which Southerners lived through and participated in.

34.
American Counterpoint: Slavery and Racism in the North-South Dialogue (1971)
by C. Vann Woodward

Woodward, a critic of the South but not afflicted by Northern righteousness, presents much neglected information about the Northern history of "racism."

35.

Walter Clark: Fighting Judge (1944)
by Aubrey Lee Brooks

In 1861 Walter Clark was a 15-year-old cadet drilling Confederate recruits. When he passed away in 1924 he was the beloved Chief Justice of North Carolina. There are a number of good biographies of Southerners in "the New South" and the Progressive Era but there is still a vast amount to be understood about that period of Southern history. Walter Clark's life is a good place to start. For the same period see *Zeb Vance: Champion of Personal Freedom* by Glenn Tucker, covering Vance's postwar career as a national figure.

36.

The Poetry of Sidney Lanier

Sidney Lanier (1842—1881) of Georgia was an outstanding lyric poet and one of the South's leading literary voices in the later 19th century. He was a Confederate soldier whose incarceration in a Yankee POW camp wrecked his health and brought his death at the age of 39. He is most noted for his poems celebrating the land of Georgia, like "The Marshes of Glynn" and "Song of the

Chattahoochee." Lanier's postwar years were a struggle until he was appointed in 1873 as a professor at the new Johns Hopkins University, which was open to Southerners. He was also the author of children's books, was a pioneer in improvements in classroom education, and was a concert level flutist and composer. Lanier's works are available in many print and online editions. Lanier's life and promise, like Henry Timrod's, was truncated by the invasion of their homeland, with a loss to world culture.

37.
Tales of Uncle Remus (written 1876—1906)
by Joel Chandler Harris

The Atlanta newspaper editor Harris (1848—1908) began the tales of Uncle Remus as newspaper and magazine sketches. They became immensely popular across America and the world. Harris was personally knowledgeable of and inspired by firsthand acquaintance with African Americans. His work is now disparaged, of course, but he saved much folklore that might have otherwise been lost. The African American writer James Weldon Johnson called Harris's work "the greatest body of folklore ever produced in America." Uncle Remus was no revolutionary, but he was a good and wise man, though humble in his time and circumstances. Br'er Rabbit, Br'er Fox, the Briar Patch and the Tar Baby are everlasting features of American culture. The Uncles Remus stories were translated into 40 languages and won praise from Mark Twain, Rudyard Kipling and many contemporary and later writers. *The Complete Tales of Uncle Remus* has been published in many editions. The Disney film "Song of the South," was about Uncle Remus but seems to be no longer in favour. My copy was bought from a private seller and has Japanese subtitles.

38.

American Populism: A Social History, 1877—1898
by Robert C. McMath

Most works on the late 19th century Populist movement, a farmers' uprising against crony capitalism that forms a significant part of American history, concentrate on the Midwestern movement. McMath's book is good on the vital Southern aspects. Populism could hardly have gained any traction except for the South.

39.

The Texas Rangers:
A Century of Frontier Defense (1935)
by Walter Prescott Webb

The Southerners who created and expanded Texas in the 19th century had dangerous borders on three sides. Besides the usual frontier banditry, they faced hostile Mexicans and the fiercest Indian nations in North America. The U.S. Army was of little help, especially during Reconstruction when General Sheridan, the foreign-born military governor, deliberately neglected frontier defense out of his hatred of Texans. The Texans were responsible for their own safety and civilisation. The Texas historian Webb tells here a truly epic story of heroism under the harshest conditions. For more on the author see *The Old South: 50 Essential Books*, no. 31.

40.

In Ole Virginia (1887)
and *The Burial of the Guns* (1894)
by Thomas Nelson Page

The Virginian Page (1853-1922) was a Southern writer who won national recognition as well as fame and fortune in the later 19th and early 20th centuries. He might be considered the most important literary voice of the South in his time. Page's boyhood was spent near Richmond during the War and in an impoverished Reconstruction. His stories appeared in Northern journals, became immensely popular, and were subsequently collected in books. (Page's complete works comprise 14 volumes.) His early stories, of which "Marse Chan" (*In Ole Virginia*) is perhaps the best known, portrayed an earlier, happier South in which affection and loyalty between masters and servants prevailed. This portrayal is now derided, but as the literary scholar Jay B. Hubbell wrote, Page's view was a painting and not a photograph. If he did not tell the whole story, his painting reflected things that really existed. His was very much the literature of reconciliation which Northerners, disgusted with Reconstruction, devoured enthusiastically. Page's success was a product of Northern readership, perhaps because he portrayed an earlier time that was better than the ugly period in which he wrote. In his later stories, like those collected in *The Burial of the Guns*, Page wrote realistically about his own time. His nonfiction book, *The Old South* (1892), on the state of the South and Southern history at the time, is worth a look for those wanting to understand this era of Southern and national life. Like many "reactionary" Southerners of the postwar period, he was a liberal in the best sense, defending labour and immigrants. President Woodrow Wilson appointed Page as U.S. ambassador to Italy where he served ably during the tumultuous World War I period.

41.

Old Judge Priest
by Irvin S. Cobb

Irvin Shrewsbury Cobb (1876—1944) was a Kentuckian who achieved great success in New York journalism. He was said to be the best-paid reporter of the time and covered World War I and many major news events. He even acted in a few movies. But he was best known as a humourist, with 60 books and countless other publications. Although his "Judge Priest" stories were first collected in a book in 1915, most were written earlier. Judge Priest is a wise, honourable, and benevolent ex-Confederate involved in the life of a Kentucky town in the later 19th century. He was the subject of two John Ford movies: "Judge Priest" (1934), starring

Will Rogers, and "The Sun Shines Bright" (1953) with Charles Winninger.

42.

True Grit by Charles Portis
& *The Searchers*
by Alan LeMay

Most "Westerns," books and movies, indeed most of the history of the American frontier, are really the stories of Southerners who have moved into new and difficult territory. These books are such —set in the frontiers of the Indian Territory (Oklahoma) and West Texas and about Southern people coping with "the West." That point is often lost because such "Southerns" have been absorbed into generic American "Westerns." But don't forget these are stories of *Southerners* enduring postwar conditions. The heroic West is mostly Southern. The Northern West is mostly sodbusters, Yankee school marms, snowstorms, and McCormick reapers. The *True Grit* adventures of young Mattie Ross and one-eyed Marshal Rooster Cogburn in the post-Confederate Indian territory west of Arkansas are perhaps eternally memorable in American culture. *True Grit* has been called "one of the great American novels."

The book became one of John Wayne's best films (1969) and was followed up by "Rooster Cogburn" (1975) in which Wayne tangles with the Yankee schoolmarm Katherine Hepburn. (You can safely skip the 2010 remake and associated book in which the actors are Hollywood types without a clue about the people they are representing and in which Mattie's Christianity is suppressed.) *The Searchers* is a grimly realistic picture of real Texas people surviving on their long-ravaged western frontier.

43.

"Man Over Money": The Southern Populist
Critique of American Capitalism
by Bruce Palmer

The mainstream historiography of the post-Reconstruction South has been largely based upon the C. Vann Woodward classic, *Reunion and Reaction* (1951). Woodward suggested that Reconstruction ended in an 1876 deal between Republicans and Southern elites to collaborate in a coalition against popular democracy. Woodward wrote at a time when a large theme of New Deal liberalism was that a coalition of Republicans and Southern Democrats were thwarting the liberal agenda. His history was clearly a product of his times, and the thesis of *Reunion and Reaction* is questionable. Ex-Confederates and Southern Democrats displayed many different political tendencies during the "New South" period. Even when the agreed with the Republicans it was not necessarily for the same greedy reasons. The persistence of Jeffersonian thought, though in an attenuated form, was a major factor in Southern political motivations. This is an intensive, somewhat critical, but largely sympathetic study.

44.

Library of Southern Literature
(16 vols., 1906-1913)
Edited by Joel Chandler Harris, *et al.*

These beautiful and well-done volumes trace Southern literature from its beginnings in the 17th century to the time of publication. They give biographies and illustrative extracts of Southern writers. They represent a consciousness of the continuity and quality of Southern culture. The set can be obtained, and individual volumes, any of which is easy and pleasant reading, are always popping up in the used book market.

45.

Life and Speeches of Thomas E. Watson (1908)

No guide to writing of the "New South" era can omit Thomas Edward Watson (1856-1922) of Georgia. Watson was an eloquent maverick and very influential in his time, especially in the magazines that he edited and in his speeches. Service in the U.S. House and Senate were the least of his accomplishments. He flourished as a lawyer, historian, editor, publisher, and public figure. He was a leader of the Populist Party, a farmers' revolt against the existing crony capitalist regime, being its vice-presidential nominee in 1896 and its last presidential candidate in 1904 and 1908. Watson vigourously represented Southern Jeffersonianism and "the common man," with learned opposition to Big Business, railroads, banks, professional politicians, and the duopoly of establishment Democrats and Republicans who differed in few significant ways. He was the author of a half dozen books, including biographies of Thomas Jefferson and Andrew Jackson and on French history. Watson has fallen out of favour because of his racial and religious views. They were common for the time but much more vigourously expressed than was usual.

His statue was erected on the grounds of the Georgia capitol, but has since been moved to a park. I am glad I had my picture taken in its original place. The volume listed here contains some autobiographical memoirs, comments on Watson by other prominent men, and a collection of his speeches for various occasions. A collection of Watson's Jeffersonian articles and speeches is badly needed as a help to understanding his times.

46.

The Bostonians (1886)
by Henry James

Henry James (1843-1916) is regarded on both sides of the Atlantic as one of the greatest fiction writers in English of all times. (Although for us plain folk he is something of an acquired taste, like opera.) *The Bostonians* is well worth a Southern reading list. A young ex-Confederate from Mississippi comes to New York in hopes of making a living. He pays a visit of duty to a lady cousin in Boston where he meets "the girl of his dreams." There follows a contest between Boston reformers who want to use the young lady, who has a mesmerizing stage presence, as an orator for feminism and the Southerner, who wants her for his wife. This time, the Southerner wins. Though defeated and poor, he is alive and vital, a great contrast to the dessicated Boston society living on the abstract remnants of abolition glory. The 1984 movie version is pretty faithful.

47.

Christmas Night in the Quarters and Other Poems (1917)
by Irwin Russell

Irwin Russell (1853—1879) was a Mississippi prodigy who died in an epidemic at the age of 26. He began writing for *Scribner's Magazine* in 1876, but, like Henry Timrod, did not have his poems in a book collection until after his death. Russell's poetry, with accompanying drawings, portrayed African Americans' speaking within their own culture and in their own dialect. Russell's approach to his subjects was respectful and experts at the time considered the dialect sound. Of course, such an approach is now *verboten*. He is considered a forerunner of Joel Chandler Harris and Thomas Nelson Page in bringing black Americans into literature. And Russell's writings have respect for the wisdom of unlettered African Americans.

48.

Claude Kitchin and the Wilson War Policies
by Alex M. Arnett

Kitchin was a member of the U.S. House of Representatives from Nathaniel Macon's Old Republican district in North Carolina. He sacrificed a leadership role in the House in order to oppose Woodrow Wilson's machinations to get the U.S. involved in World War I. For other Southern leaders who opposed American imperialism and internationalism see *Tom Watson: Agrarian Rebel* by C. Vann Woodward and *Pitchfork Ben Tillman* by Francis Butler Simkins.

49.

Yankee Empire: Aggressive Abroad and Despotic at Home (2018)
by James Ronald Kennedy & Walter Donald Kennedy

In 1866, in response to the British historian Acton, General R.E. Lee wrote that he feared the newly consolidated national government which had replaced the old Union would likely become "aggressive abroad and despotic at home," like other such governments had too often become in history. The Kennedys, well-known for many good books examining America from a Southern viewpoint, have taken Lee's unexampled wisdom to heart. In a historical survey that is startlingly relevant to today, they trace the history of American imperialism. The conquest of the South for the benefit of state capitalism is the first exhibit. It continued with the illegal annexation of Hawaii, the brutal suppression of Philippine independence, and armed interventions in the Caribbean and South America —all, like the conquest of the South, motivated by greed but covered by a pretense of doing good to people less enlightened than the Yankee. (The Republican party platform of 1900 avowed that the Filipinos should be crushed for resisting, like the Southern rebels, the benefits bestowed by the greatest government on earth.) Any American who is concerned about the worldwide military empire of the U.S. today will profit greatly from this eloquent and hard-hitting examination of its origins.

50.
Reader's Choice

This reader's guide covers a long, complicated, and controversial period of history. Undoubtedly we have missed significant works and will be delighted for you to let us know at **shotwell@sc.rr.com** of good choices we have neglected.

ABOUT THE AUTHOR

DR. CLYDE N. WILSON is Emeritus Distinguished Professor of History of the University of South Carolina, where he served from 1971 to 2006. He holds a Ph.D. from the University of North Carolina at Chapel Hill. Wilson was editor of the 28-volume edition of *The Papers of John C. Calhoun* which has received high praise. He is author or editor of more than 20 other books and over 700 articles, essays, and reviews in a variety of books and journals, and has lectured all over the U.S. and in Europe.

Dr. Wilson directed 17 doctoral dissertations, a number of which have been published. His books written or edited include *Why the South Will Survive, Carolina Cavalier: The Life and Mind of James Johnston Pettigrew, The Essential Calhoun,* three volumes of *The Dictionary of Literary Biography* on American Historians, *From Union to Empire: Essays in the Jeffersonian Tradition, Defending Dixie: Essays in Southern History and Culture, Chronicles of the South,* and *The Yankee Problem.*

Dr. Wilson is founding director of the Society of Independent Southern Historians; former president of the St. George Tucker Society for Southern Studies; recipient of the Bostick Prize for Contributions to South Carolina Letters, the first annual John Randolph Society Lifetime Achievement Award, and of the Robert E. Lee Medal of the Sons of Confederate Veterans. He is M.E. Bradford Distinguished Professor of the Abbeville Institute; Contributing Editor of *Chronicles: A Magazine of American Culture*; founding dean of the Stephen D. Lee Institute, educational arm of the Sons of Confederate Veterans; and co-founder of Shotwell Publishing.

Dr. Wilson has two grown daughters, an excellent son-in-law, and two outstanding grandsons. He lives in the Dutch Fork of South Carolina, not far from the Santee Swamp where Francis Marion and his men rested between raids on the first invader.

AVAILABLE FROM SHOTWELL PUBLISHING

If you enjoyed this book, perhaps some of our other titles will pique your interest. The following titles are now available at most major online retailers. Enjoy!

JOYCE BENNETT

+ *Maryland, My Maryland: The Cultural Cleansing of a Small Southern State*

GARRY BOWERS

+ *Slavery and the Civil War*

JERRY BREWER

+ *Dismantling the Republic*

ANDREW P. CALHOUN, JR., ED.

+ *My Own Darling Wife: Letters From a Confederate Volunteer* [John Francis Calhoun]

JOHN CHODES

- *Segregation: Federal Policy or Racism?*
- *Washington's KKK: The Union League During Southern Reconstruction*

PAUL C. GRAHAM

- *Confederaphobia: An American Epidemic*
- *When the Yankees Come: Former South Carolina Slaves Remember Sherman's Invasion* (Voices from the Dust I)

JOSEPH JAY

- *Sacred Conviction: The South's Stand for Biblical Authority*

JAMES R. KENNEDY

- *Dixie Rising: Rules for Rebels*

JAMES R. & WALTER D. KENNEDY

- *Punished with Poverty: The Suffering South*
- *Yankee Empire: Aggressive Abroad and Despotic At Home*

PHILIP LEIGH

- *The Devil's Town: Hot Spring During the Gangster Era*
- *U.S. Grant's Failed Presidency*

48

MICHAEL MARTIN

- *Southern Grit: Sensing the Siege at Petersburg*

LEWIS LIBERMAN

- *Snowflake Buddies: ABCs for Leftism for Kids!*

CHARLES T. PACE

- *Lincoln As He Really Was*
- *Southern Independence. Why War?*

JAMES RUTLEDGE ROESCH

- *From Founding Fathers to Fire Eaters: The Constitutional Doctrine of States' Rights in the Old South*

KIRKPATRICK SALE

- *Emancipation Hell: The Tragedy Wrought By Lincoln's Emancipation Proclamation*

KAREN STOKES

- *A Legion of Devils: Sherman in South Carolina*
- *Carolina Love Letters*

JOHN VINSON

- *Southerner, Take Your Stand!*

HOWARD RAY WHITE

- *Understanding Creation and Evolution*

WALTER KIRK WOOD

- *Beyond Slavery: The Northern Romantic
  Nationalist Origins of America's Civil War*

CLYDE N. WILSON

- *Annals of the Stupid Party: Republicans
  Before Trump* (The Wilson Files 3)
- *Lies My Teacher Told Me: The True History
  of the War for Southern Independence*
- *Nullification: Reclaiming Consent of the
  Governed* (The Wilson Files 2)
- *The Old South: 50 Essential Books* (Southern
  Reader's Guide I)
- *The War Between the States: 60 Essential* Books
  (Southern Reader's Guide II)
- *The Yankee Problem: An American Dilemma*
  (The Wilson Files 1)

———————————

GREEN ALTAR BOOKS

-Literary Imprint-

CATHARINE SAVAGE BROSMAN

♦ *An Aesthetic Education & Other Stories*

RANDALL IVEY

♦ *A New England Romance & Other SOUTHERN Stories*

JAMES EVERETT KIBLER

♦ *Tiller* (Clay Bank County, IV)

THOMAS MOORE

♦ *A Fatal Mercy*

KAREN STOKES

♦ *Belles: A Carolina Romance*
♦ *Honor in the Dust*
♦ *The Immortals*
♦ *The Soldier's Ghost: A Tale of Charleston*

GOLD-BUG
-Mystery & Suspense Imprint-

MICHAEL ANDREW GRISSOM

+ *Billie Jo*

BRANDI PERRY

+ *Splintered: A New Orleans Tale*

MARTIN L. WILSON

+ *To Jekyll and Hide*

Free Book Offer

Sign-up for new release notification and receive a **FREE** downloadable edition of *LIES MY TEACHER TOLD ME: THE TRUE HISTORY OF THE WAR FOR SOUTHERN INDEPENDENCE* by Dr. Clyde N. Wilson by visiting FreeLiesBook.com or by texting the word "Dixie" to 345345. You can always unsubscribe and keep the book, so you've got nothing to lose!

Southern Without Apology.

CPSIA information can be obtained
at www.ICGtesting.com
Printed in the USA
LVHW040752180920
666448LV00001B/76

9 781947 660236